Gallery Books
Editor Peter Fallon

AGAINST THE CLOCK

Derek Mahon

AGAINST THE CLOCK

Gallery Books

Against the Clock
is first published
simultaneously in paperback
and in a clothbound edition
on 17 August 2018.

The Gallery Press
Loughcrew
Oldcastle
County Meath
Ireland

www.gallerypress.com

ISBN 978 1 91133 742 3 *paperback*
       978 1 91133 743 0 *clothbound*

Against the Clock receives financial assistance
from the Arts Council.

Contents

Against the Clock *page* 11
Horizons 13
Bridges 14
The Flying Boats 15
Ninth Wave 16
Palinurus 17
Montaigne 18
At the Strand Café 19
Olympia 20
A Clearing 21
Dead of Night 22
Botany 23
At the Window 24
Jersey and Guernsey 25
Rain Shadows 27
Working Conditions 30
Stuff 31
Data 32
Ebb Tide 33
To Anne Brontë 34
A Birthday 35
Mythistorema 36
Rising Late 38
A Bright Patch 40
A Full Moon in May 42
Stardust 44
Howe Strand 45
Homage to Joseph Kell 47
Cork in Old Photographs 48
The Rain Forest 49
Triad for Shane MacGowan 51
   1 A Rainy Night in Soho
   2 Fairytale of New York
   3 Brought Up to Agitate
To Hugh Haughton Retiring 53
An Age of Revolution 54

On a Drowned Girl 55
On Swimming in Lakes and Rivers 56
Brave New World 58
Trump Time 59
Ophelia 61
Ivy 63
Being a Dog 65
Thing Theory 67
Salisbury Avenue 69
A Dove in the House 70
A North Light 72
Domestic Interior 74
Woodpigeons at the Grove 76

Acknowledgements 79

for Sarah

Against the Clock

Writing against the clock, the flying calendar,
not to a regular but to a final deadline
(life is short and time, the great reminder,
closes the file of new poems in line
for the printer and binder),

you think of those who wrestled with language
until dementia or whatever struck —
old lads, old girls, the poets of old age
who scribbled on at the unfinished work
with undiminished courage.

Don't give in or give up. Sophocles, obviously,
who wrote *Colonus* in his ninetieth year
is our exemplar; and persistent Ovid,
relegated for life to a distant shore,
who fought on for a reprieve.

So many exiles! So many reprobates! —
for whom, to their credit, it was never over:
Dante and Coleridge, Hugo, Whitman, Yeats
and persecuted, proud Akhmatova
who sang to the black nights.

There are those grim moments when you think
contemporary paper games too daft for you,
not serious, and real values on the blink —
a naff culture not worth contributing to,
time to go back on the drink,

and the old faces turn to you in disgust:
'You're here for the one purpose and one only,
to give us of your best even if your best
is rubbish and your personal testimony
of little general interest.

11

'You thought you'd done, the uneven output
finished at last, but that wasn't the end,
was it, since we're obliged to stick it out
until the pen falls from the trembling hand;
so just get on with it.'

Horizons

Night wind — a continual, baffled aspirate —
wanders the water like a vagrant spirit
seeking repose but there is no repose
till morning, when the tide withdraws
from exposed depths to the south-west
with its imaginary Islands of the Blest.

A straight line, wherever the edge may be,
confines and also opens up the sea
to ancient shipwreck, drowned forest,
lost continents and nuclear waste.
You hear a different music of the spheres
depending where you stand on these quiet shores.

Relatedly, beyond the blue horizon,
beyond the rising and declining sun
are more horizons, and among real waves
the line recedes to infinite alternatives
before the final hot sand or pack ice.
Nobody clears the same horizon twice.

Same thing with time. When you were twenty-one
you took it for granted you would die young
as genius should. Now that you're seventy-five,
sails idly fluttering, but still alive,
you sit becalmed, imagining the many
horizons past and those to come, if any.

Bridges

The narrow road bridge up at Cushendun
was where we gathered when the day was done
back in the fifties. Peaty water raced
past trailing branches, tackle, and dispersed
to late-summer tides at the sand spit.
Stars shone in the leaves at night.

Girls on the bridge, men at the nets, seagulls
planing in and out of the Antrim hills —
it was one of those lasting primal scenes
in sparkling definition, glimpsed again
from boardwalks on the Thames and Seine,
high bridges over gorges and ravines

and the one linking Crane's two shores to prove
bright theorem and entelechy from above
dockside, freighter and barge, the brief
pedestrianism of the quotidian life —
sun on a hundred windows, icy wings,
a rainbow shining in a flight of strings.

The Flying Boats

Our wired-up, tensile hearts are set
on the slow-starting harbourflights.com,
a new outfit based at Mountshannon, Co. Clare;
but they haven't got their act together yet,
so we're stuck here with the manufacturer
like adolescents bored at home.

Giddy by choice, we'd much prefer
to be flying in open water, sailing on air
or both at once, sky water crowded with clouds:
the ambiguous is our element, the binary, yin and yang.
(Short Bros. thought of this in our design
and fashioned us like halcyon birds.)

Twin-engined, rocked uncertainly,
we sit tight for the airstrip of the sea
dreaming low flight, our shadows on the waves —
wave-conscious, conscious of the sand and soil.
Not for us high gleam and vapour trail.
We're the half-hidden alternatives

like disregarded, obsolete things;
but ours is the magic of real *flying boats*
you find in the legends and folk literatures.
Aeolian harps, old toys, lost causes, startling futures,
we're waiting for the sea beneath our floats,
the ocean wind beneath our wings.

Ninth Wave

Sun water creams on the hot sand.
As she surfs in, alone and self-contained,
borne strenuously ashore on the ninth wave,
an old man watches from his shady cove
fondly and even more than fondly:
'There is one story and one story only.'

Graves, I only repeat what you were saying
in your own whimsical voice, in your own day,
while you were here among the rocks and cottages —
that this one has been surfing down the ages
on the same wave, in the same foam as when
life first arose at the tideline.

We give her credit at the very least.
Haunted by death, lost love, a nightmare past,
indictments of ourselves, what should we do
with these inheritances but write them through
and sing the praises of our only nurse
in gratitudes of prose and verse?

Palinurus

Condemned to linger in the years ahead
with other souls of the unburied dead
rustling like autumn leaves blown
to the cold roar of smoky Acheron,
we waited there, so many leaves,
so many shadows of our former selves.

A seasoned helmsman, eyes fixed on the night
but sprinkled with a starry dew, sight
dim with somnolence, I'd relaxed my grip;
unnoticed by the rest I slept and slipped
into a dark sea calmer than most,
to be washed up on an unfamiliar coast.

Was there a reason? Many theories fit:
I had a blackout on the night I quit,
Juno required the forfeit of a life
so that the many might be safe,
I'd lost faith in Aeneas and this quick
defection seemed the simplest course; in fact,

wanting no more of the great expedition
I chose obscurity and isolation —
childish perhaps but there you are.
On an unfriendly, now a friendly shore
I lie at last in a grave above the sea,
my bad name a notorious promontory.

Montaigne

Que sçais-je?

Since lately I renounced administration
to spend my time in idle speculation
I've been astonished by the fantasies
an open mind can spin on its dark days;
but a hoof clicks below and an autumn sun
dazzles the live flow of the Dordogne.

I can do nothing without gaiety —
still there despite the death of Boétie.
If one book bores me I pick up another,
skimming and skipping. I would rather
shit like a gent than trouble my digestion
tackling a merely theoretic question.

Some have withdrawn in hopes of a mystique,
others in horror at the great mistake
of this mad century, its religious hate.
Knowing yourself you know the human fate.
What do *I* know? Only immediate things.
I think and write as the bird sings;

for mine is a lazy, self-amusing style,
not grim and purposeful as at Port-Royal.
A thought comes like a raindrop, a slow phrase
like a cloud formation or a September breeze.
I make nature my study as I grow old,
unknowing to the last, in the known world.

At the Strand Café

Ab initio
a tremulous string or two
sent out a sound wave to the infinite dark,
a hum or 'hmm', and an electric spark
set off the almighty row,
an echo now.

The first word
spoken, albeit unheard,
turned on the lights and made the oceans heave,
throwing up organisms that gasped and strove —
with other vital signs
along these lines.

Now look at us,
in this post-diluvian space
with our smartphones and our personal computers.
Our table looks on the mild face of the waters
where 'God' moved and ordained
time out of mind.

We've been for a swim
in the salt, original slime,
clean now, and tonight we dine out at the Wrixons'.
Who wouldn't endorse our fancy predilections?
Who these days would forgo
the lives we know?

Far be it from me
to doubt the authority
of evolution; but I think I go
with the theory that a knowing *cogito*,
some spirit, spoke the word
and then retired.

Olympia

We commune, she
and I, in silent privacy,
ribbon and paper glimmering. I wait,
she waits, for a first word to communicate
itself with a hesitant beat
to the white sheet.

A second word,
a short pause, then a third;
and now there comes a fluent stream of them.
The two of us together find a rhythm.
So we begin the dance
of keys, the trance

of composition.
Quick and slow, we fashion
what was demanding to be said in words.
A sumptuous black register records
the notes of the concerto.
On we go,

clickety-click
(each imprint an antique
ever so slightly out of the true as if
handwritten, as if with its own personal life
stretching back to a past
lost in the mist,

old dust and fluff
hiding with other stuff
in the dark places), page after rackety page,
two crotchety relics of a previous age
jazzing it up again as
in the great days.

A Clearing

A clearing in the wood
beyond technology, with two
car doors disintegrating in a ditch;
a listening light, domain of fox and witch
and, stiff with sudden tension, you
who dubiously intrude,

fondly imagining
like someone in a fairy story
strange beings — *sídhe*, *fíanna*, dwarves, elves —
will part the leafy boughs to show themselves,
to shed light on the mystery
and let the magic in.

The glade, an open space
alive with immanent potential, pours
impersonal warmth into your narrow field
of sense; but something vital is withheld.
You wait, but nothing notable occurs
in this mysterious place —

or seems to occur, although
a wood-wide web is hard at work
reporting on your mischievous invasion
while secret presences obscured by sun,
revealed by shade, define the dark
and shine with their own glow.

What on earth shall we do
with this silent conventicle?
Install a picnic table, a building site?
No, this is where the angel will alight.
Just let it be, let be, until
the avatar is due.

Dead of Night

Arc lamps so bright tonight the thrushes sing
as though at daybreak or the start of spring
thinking it's sunrise, and in fun or fright
pursue their thing at dead of night
in light of or perhaps in spite of it —

a pop group piping in the branches, one
clear blackbird noticeable above the din,
not like McCartney's learning how to fly
with broken wing and sunken eye,
but loud and clear in its anxiety.

He'd rather be presaging lousy weather —
a downpour or a storm, one or the other;
but the blaze gets him going, the gold beak
wide open with a frightened shriek
in a far, hidden corner of the park.

Not for the lying light and not for us
he sings, distinctive in the midnight chorus,
but for the living shadows whited out,
his fierce song an indignant shout
in the bright piercing dead of night and light.

Fitzwilliam Square

Botany

Wildflowers familiar once to 'country folk'
we only recognize from the botany book.
I couldn't identify (say) tormentil,
eyebright or scabious, not until
I've checked the pictures on the page
where I first make the acquaintance
of self-heal, heartsease, leafy spurge —
these never to be known at a quick glance.

At the Window

The bird flying up at the windowpane
aspired to the blue sky reflected in it
but learned the hard truth and flew off again.
Was it a finch, a blue tit or a linnet?
I couldn't quite identify the strain.

Checking a pocket guide to get it right
(*The Birds of Ireland*, illustrated text)
I note the precise graphic work and definite
descriptions there, and yet I'm still perplexed.
I only glimpsed the bird in busy flight:

a bit like a goldfinch, like the captive one
perched on a rail, by Rembrandt's young disciple,
except for the colouring, blue, yellow and green.
A tit so, one of those from the bird table
who whirr at hanging nuts and grain.

Off he flew. Now there's a mist out there
and a mist in here that wouldn't interest him
since what he wants is sky and open air.
He's in the trees; I'm trying one more time
to find an opening in the stratosphere.

Jersey and Guernsey

(after Hugo)

1

What you can see from here is chalks and ochres,
ridged furrows radiating on ploughed acres,
a stubble field half hidden by a copse
with a few hayricks here and there, the tops
of chimneys smoking up the paintable scene;
a river, not the Seine but, mixed with brine,
the thin, slow-winding local watercourse;
on the right, northwards, ugly mounds and worse
looking as if just dumped there with a spade;
a former chapel with its spire beside
a stand of crooked elms. One notices,
on looking closer, their impatient faces
scolding the north wind for its derisive
impudence. So much for the perspective.
An old cart sits and rusts next to my entrance
and there before me is a vast expanse
of deeply breathing salt water: the sea!
   A few fowl, showing off their golden finery,
gabble beneath the window, and a song
comes from a grain loft in the island tongue.
Up the lane lives an ancient ropemaker
loudly at work as the thick weave gets thicker,
the hemp twisted around his twisted loins.
Bewildering breezes blow and the sun shines:
I could walk for ever in this open space.
Book-bearing pupils envy my easy ways
in the rented schoolhouse lodgings where I stay
like a big boy on an extended holiday,
hearing for hours on end the faint murmur
of children reading aloud on the ground floor.
   A stream flows, in the fresh air a finch goes by;

so, giving thanks, I live from day to day
peacefully, in my own good time, and spend
it writing, always thinking of you, dear friend.
I listen to the young ones and, at rare
moments, watch an imposing ship stand clear
beyond the gables of the tranquil town
perhaps for a long passage, heading down
to the ocean with its wings spread, wind-driven
which last night sheltered in a quiet haven.
Neither the tears of parents, fears of wives,
the dark shadow of rocks beneath the waves
nor the gulls' agitated importunity
can hold it back from the demanding sea.

2

Sun on the eyes, clear voices, open windows,
St Peter's chimes creating quite a din.
Sea bathers shout: *No, nearer; farther. No,
right there!* Songbirds are chirping, Jenny too.
George calls her, cocks crow, and a builder's spade
scrapes somewhere. Horses pass by on the road.
Thrash of a scythe clearing a field; the gruff
mumble of men re-tiling a slate roof.
Port noises, whistle of steam-driven machinery.
Gusts of band music; cheers down at the quay.
French spoken here: *Bonjour, merci.* I'm late
rising, for (look!) here comes my favourite
robin now, cheeping at a window ledge.
Uproar of hammers from a distant forge.
Waves flap, and a steamer wheezes breezily;
enter a fly, the vast breath of the sea.

Rain Shadows

1

Cloud-cuckooland down there
as we descended through
layers of blustery air
from sunlit realms of blue:
grey glimpses of farm gates,
hedgerows, ghost estates.

2

Thunder drum, lightning crack,
the wind section: hill squeak
of ancient organ pipes,
a whistling wood, perhaps
remotely ringing chimes,
echoes of earlier times.

3

Cold front after cold
front in the northern world,
storm damage, your path
reduced to a wet wraith:
peculiar climate here,
same as in Nigeria.

4

A raindrop strikes a leaf
and trembles at the tip;

a globe of shining, clear
light, a falling tear,
drops to a pool beneath.
Will this never stop?

5

Ground fog, drifting smoke,
sea mist, hard knowing which,
closes the prospect down
to a mile or so, a stretch
of road, a high turf stack,
first signs of a town.

6

'Summer' but no summer
as though the ash of some
immense eruption were
circling the earth to shroud
the entire biosphere
in never-clearing cloud.

7

The fogbow, a rare show,
a blank rainbow shining
on cloud banks, but no
colour seen in the bow,
fog drops are so tiny;
only a faint white glow.

8

Darkness at noon. A room,
dim presences, rain shadows,
fog spectres, foggy dews,
an artist by lamplight:
bright paper, ink, graphite,
a sure hand in the gloom.

9

Early this morning starlit
azure for the first time
in weeks, and a pale sun
took shape on the horizon.
We think again and claim
life; now for the hard bit.

'Nasc' Immigrant Support Centre

Working Conditions

A beloved presence, the right kind of light
preferably from an eastward-facing window.
A bit of river if you can organize it,
bird life, a windbreak and some sea below,
though not vital, will be of help to you.
Now you're ready to sit down and write.

Other things will help besides of course:
a rhyme in your head or a persistent theme
that won't leave you alone and, worse,
troubles your sleep; a tendency to dream;
rapid reactions when the hunches come
and frequent practice in the art of verse.

Of use too are the work of previous ages —
philosophy, theatre, fiction — and at least
some slight knowledge of other languages
dead or alive, though the dead are best.
As for your own contemporaries, stay abreast
to avoid things already there in their pages.

Above all you will have to keep in time
with the deep rhythms, with the inconstant beat
of the life cycle, though not to the point of tedium
since you don't want to be obvious or too 'great';
but anything goes if it works, if it contribute
a howl or a whisper to the sum of wisdom.

Stuff

Woodshavings, oil and canvas, sand and stone,
atoms aswirl like barn dust in the sun,
already hold the paper, glass and artefacts
they're destined to become in a short while.
All that's required is skill, a sense of style
and a concrete devotion to the facts.

Stuff grows around us — jotter, ink and slate —
with an interior life keen to create;
the picture above the table, the cracked plate,
broken specs, defaced books on the shelves
and the stuff dreams are made of, we ourselves
whose dancing atoms share a similar fate.

Data

I'm noticing once again the singular things
I noticed as a boy: the hidden springs,
the sound of silence, nap of tablecloths,
sea taste of iodine, the scents of clothes,
raw grain of wood, a scrambling interface
of ebbing tide and incoming tide race.

Light, hot on the 'fanatical existence'
of furniture and the brightwork of kitchens,
on country garage, hen run and mown hay,
shines everything, even on the rainiest day,
with the reflected or intrinsic glow
of an intentional world we think we know —

the inert, potential force of things material.
Our knowledge instrumental, our facts unreal
because unlived, unfelt, what can we use
for wisdom but these fierce realities?
We don't need telescopes to appreciate
the silent music of the sky at night;

nor do we need computers to contemplate
that morphic resonance where swifts migrate
in close formation from a river mouth
knowing by instinct when to travel south,
also by instinct to retrace their flight
when hawthorn is in leaf, its flowers alight.

Ebb Tide

The riddles of the sand — a field of wrack
and shifting shingle left by the ebb tide,
new dispositions every time — avoid
consistency, and when the sea draws back
everything, even our confidence, has died
in an archaic stench of primal mud.

Ah yes, but this is where new life begins,
that 'inter-tidal zone' where the sun warms
vast cloud reflections on a moist expanse
beneath the sky: a place of origins,
a fertile space for the evolving forms
like us with our own conscious ignorance.

To Anne Brontë

Remembering Arthur's cronies in the *Tenant*
I know you wouldn't want to know me, Anne,
but I came upon your plaque above the harbour
on an exposed clifftop in Scarborough
and thought about your happy visits there
in wild commotions of the salty air.

I love your drawing, a self-portrait surely,
of a young woman gazing out to sea,
shading her eyes as day springs in the east,
your vision of release from the bombastic
new rich of a 'manufacturing' town;
sails in the bay, the rippling sand at dawn.

It's there you're buried, not at grisly Haworth
riddled with dogma and contagion, earth
enclosing you who dreamed a generous heaven —
a faith sustained, sustaining like the proven
benefits of earthly wind and peony,
alms of the sun, a last glimpse of the sea.

A Birthday

I know we shouldn't write paternalistic
poems to our daughters in this generation,
for even the simple fact of being a dad
leaves one wide open to the imputation
of soppiness or something equally bad
like deference to the feminine mystique;

but let me mark this rather *seerious* date
with a few lines, although I don't deny
I think of you as a young one even yet,
a cheeky child who shouted 'Fiddlesticks!'
at a strange gent, and chanted 'Paranoia'.
You were a vocalist from the age of six

though your real music wasn't rock and pop
but *bel canto* and parody. Listening hard
to 'Katy Mahon Sings Purcell' on tape
I marvel at how such a new-fledged bird
achieved such easy confidence of tone
when she was only twenty or twenty-one.

And now you're forty (phew!), yourself a mum,
a 'single mother' since your gentil knight
was roughly carried off into the night
leaving a young widow; but when you come
to visit, the wise child is there once more
if older and slightly wiser than before.

What can I wish for you but happier days
to make up for the crisis you came through
with such resilience? Always here for you,
I watch your life unfold in phases, always
picturing that maid in a flowery smock
whose recent photo rests against the clock.

Mythistorema

(for Charles Tyrrell)

Dark in the dark entrance of a mindshaft
(gunpowder, picks and shovels, copper veins),
miners climbed daily down to their hard graft —
locals and tin-men brought in from Penwith
ten generations ago; and what remains?
A copper-mine museum, a ghost of myth.

Lanyon's 'Lost Mine' with its decrepit timbers,
its grey rubble and dying crimson embers
of an old life, reflects a time when ground
was blown apart without a qualm. A wised-up
part of the landscape, we consumed landscape
in the days before ecology came around.

We try to grasp it but the past dies back
to a grainy line-up of old photographs.
Eurydice retreads the downward path
while Orpheus comes out at a rough door
to disused engine houses, chimney stacks
and a full moon shining on ruined Kôr.

The struck lyre ripples as a stricken voice
sings out to heather and bog asphodel,
sandstone peninsula, island, sea and sky.
The very choughs are silent, a cliff face
listens amazed to the euphonious wail;
the rocks relax their ancient obduracy.

A happy outcome really, each one saved
for a harmonious fate befitting both —
she, beyond tears, definitively received
into the infinite; he, having failed

in his heroic bid, condemned thenceforth
to sing on in the clear light of the world.

What of the miners? When the pits shut down
they took off for Montana and Colorado.
Eurydice, had she much of mourning? No:
Orpheus, still in love with her lost shadow,
soon came to a sticky end. Now everyone
whispers together in the dim fields below.

Allihies

Rising Late

Sun on the eyes, clear voices, open window,
birdsong; ponies clop by on the road below.
Whine of a chainsaw, the recurrent roar
of power tools from a building site next door
with crashing, rumbling, safety beep and buzz.
A seagull shadow flickers; harbour noise;
a honking coaster backs out from the quay.
Enter a fly, the vast breath of the sea.

Waking mid-morning to a springlike new year
and a new age of unbeauty, rage and fear
much like the previous one, I wonder if
a time could ever come when human life,
relieved of ego and finance, might thrive
on the mere fact of existence. A naive
hope, but naive hopes are what unchain
the doors when January comes round again.

Such tiny houses, such enormous skies!
The vast sea-breath reminds us, even these days
as even more oil and junk slosh in the waves,
the future remains open to alternatives.
A stretch in the evenings as returning light
slowly expands. Crocuses, yellow and white,
have sprung up overnight under the pines.
It just keeps happening; life always finds

somewhere to whisper, thought a place to grow
even while the poets fade, as now they do
this winter, taking with them when they die
their quotient of soul, song and singularity,
their fierce resistance to the philistinism;
those acute angles, inspired algorithms,
that first-day-of-creation point of view
old Hugo in his Guernsey exile knew.

Best skies at first light, but I don't do dawn
no more. The enchantment has already gone
when I rise, creaking, to the noise outside,
phenomenal moment of cup, pine and cloud,
the things themselves and the idea of them
embodied there. Plato (*Timaeus*): 'Time
is the moving picture of eternity' —
in love, the pair of them, or said to be.

Salvation lies in love of the simple thing
such as our complex poets used to sing:
a rose, a table with its magic glow,
the ideal forms they body forth also.
I would become, in the time left to me,
the servant of a restored reality —
chalks and ochres, birdsong, harbour lights,
the longer days and the short summer nights.

A Bright Patch

Over my shoulder each
of these May mornings early the sun slides in
hoping to watch a scribbled line begin
and take shape on the page, in a bright patch,
at its own living touch.

It has been pouring down
through holes in the ozone layer its white heat
on Goa and Dubai; and now, more temperate,
dries up the remaining night dew on the lawn,
shining the birches. Sun,

you will have work to do
now, ripening the crops, warming the sea
so we can swim a bit, though your priority,
keeping the stars in order, beats the few
favours we ask of you.

Once in Washington Square
I stole a glance, no more, at your eclipse
and noticed a strange leaf-light like a glimpse
of an unknown reality, a rare
alternative in the air —

as if those staring towers,
grown dim, confronted briefly your black heart
in a gas cloud; as if those eyes could penetrate
whatever turns you on, whatever fires
yourself and the other stars.

When the rash, innocent son
of the sun god lost control of his gold chariot
the earth smoked, the seas shrank, it grew so hot,
and you whirled Icarus like a wounded pigeon
into the blue Aegean;

but we insist upon
your life-enhancing, life-giving track record.
We live by grace of the creative word, your word
as it was in the beginning, since you're the one
who woke us up at dawn.

What should we do but praise
your generosity though you reduce to ash
our towers, technology and commercial trash
in time to come? Shed light on our dark days
with your prodigious rays!

A Full Moon in May

Diana, Artemis, Astarte,
you of the many profiles, you who exercise
the same influence everywhere to our wondering gaze,
we know you as the ambiguous authority
in our dark stretch of sky.

As Artemis you enlightened
the thick-branched forest with your furious glow;
as bright Diana of the gleaming bow
you hunted stars and ruled the unquiet night
with virginal oversight.

As Cynthia, as Hecate, you seduced
the blow-in soldier poets so much feared
throughout Munster in the Elizabethan period
and drowned bemused Li Po who reached to embrace
your pale reflected face.

The oceans ebb and flow
as your residual gravity decides,
regulating the calendar and the tides.
(You used to dance like a spinning-top when new
many long aeons ago.)

A further continent,
you illuminate, early rising, our garden parties,
bobbing up like a balloon among the trees,
your engraved silver image a swung pendant,
coin fresh from the mint.

Oh, you try to behave
like a good moon, like a dutiful handmaiden
of mild demeanour, keeping your dark side hidden,
demure in your veiled phases, modestly grave
in your cloud-skirted cave;

but the old one is still there,
violent and inspirational though 'chaste
and fair', as now you drift off to the south-west
casting a wary eye on our blue sphere
below, which you used to share.

Space tourism and popular song
have made it hard to take you seriously
but you shine on — grandly, mysteriously —
your silence resonant as a struck gong
still singing, still going strong.

Stardust

Dead many a light year
beyond us, their bright eyes established here
in the anthropocentric centuries to vie
with raves and airports in high visibility,
the burnt-out stars themselves are now at rest
in clouds of mineral dust.

These were the crucible
before we came in cinders and flying rubble
to this raw shore, to crawl on its warm sands
inventing hope. (Were we out of our tiny minds?)
Once in a while we visit a beach at night
to see where we started out

and meet with starlight there.
Specks of stardust far from our proper sphere,
no more than sand grains on that infinite road,
we scan immense formations and decode
the blinking flashlamps of an old dispatch
now clearly within reach:

'Known to you as the stars,
we were your startling origin, and ours
the original substances from which you grew.
Some of that heritage we bequeathed to you
in pre-existent forms as cold as ice,
and your idea of paradise.

'You live in the world now
with its wild, hope-induced chaotic flow.
Resolve the climate problem if you dare
and change your thinking if you can. We're here
for you in the night sky you so admire
to invigilate and inspire.'

Howe Strand

A philosopher lived here in the blue house once
in love with mystery and his spirited spouse,
watching at evening where the plovers pounce
for worms, or where the lighthouse flashes twice
each ten seconds, and redirects its glance.

Wind shakes a telephone wire in fields of grain
and bangs the back door of the Strand Café.
Surf detonates at the high-water line;
for this is March, spring tide, and the geography
is painted in bold strokes that strive and strain.

Soon the first primrose and the first lark flight
to hymn the sun behind its mist of spray;
soon the first families at the caravan site,
children out on the sand and rocks each day
and gas lamps singing in the April night.

How is the question, *how* did this arise?
What obscure impulse formed from what absurd
contingencies the sights that sting our eyes,
the eyes themselves, the brainbox, and the proud
belief in our unbounded expertise?

Right now the blowing sky, a constant flux
embodied in the waves, perhaps a metaphor
of relative values and conflicting facts
with only wind and wave to settle for,
each of them piling paradox upon paradox,

neither providing any definite word,
only the white foam of a libidinous sea.
Amid cold chaos down below a bird
flies low over the wavecrests with a cry
of fright or temper. Nothing else is heard,

nothing except the taut hum of the wire,
a resonant string above the rocky fields,
and the faint music of a single star
this morning, whose high register reveals
a stir of soul stuff in the atmosphere.

It's a thin, vibrant voice we're listening to,
words indistinct in the still wintery air.
Tell me, philosopher, when she sings do you
see her as a creative force anterior
to systematic thought? I know I do.

Chaos, an order without obvious order, throws
such revelations at the shivering sand
I could believe today a spirit chose
this rich confusion in the void, its hand
still loudly evident as the daylight grows.

Homage to Joseph Kell

Ask of the gorgeous widow in the meadow
whether time stops or dashes fast forward.
It flies, of course, but the unsought reward
is that split second when you the reader
pause at a sprung rhythm or a strange word.
'The running tap casts a static shadow.'

Always already quicker than you knew,
the living river you can't enter twice
bears everything away; but, slick as ice,
an ideal stream rushes on without moving.
The whistle in the sink is a singing voice
for ever pitch-perfect, for ever new —

a blade of music as clean as sculpture,
the shadow I mean, for some things do keep,
sometimes at least, their flowing frozen shape
with noticeably soul-opening results,
and fugitive time can be made to stop
by art or artifice at any juncture.

While waiting unctuously for the widow
go fetch the tea kettle and fill it up.
Watch clear water pour from the cold tap
like a fine thing by Brancusi or another —
the line in tune, decisive, no stray drop
to wreck it or its static shadow either.

Cork in Old Photographs

(for Chris and Amy Ramsden)

The old-time snappers, heavily laden, captured
opera productions, early twentieth century,
the open trams in Grand Parade, St. Finbarre's,
bowlers and shawlies, a few motor cars,
low bridges, the wild scramble of the Lee.
(A lot of water since the cameras whirred.)

Straw hats and awnings, therefore summertime
in some of them. A clock reads five to four;
listen and soon, above the muffled roar
of work and talk, you're hearing Shandon chime.
You're back in the old days of Frank O'Connor,
of Hadji Bey, of Woodford's on the corner

and the Oyster Tavern as it used to be
before the sticky floors and slot machines,
the torture music, the inane soundtrack
of global capitalism; that harsh cacophony.
Give my head peace. Oh, take me back
to those pre-digital, pre-industrial scenes

or forward to a time of . . . There, you see?
Nothing will ever set my mind at rest,
not even this antique photography
of a lost world whose images recall
a life absorbed and self-contained, a past
already fading as the shutters fall.

The Rain Forest

Mountjoy demanded clearance
of 'difficult places', the thick woods
where non-compliance found its ancient refuge.
This done, the expropriated fugitives
took ship for warmer latitudes
or played dead for years.

Surviving forests, slighted
by the proud native eye, remain,
indigenous silent thickets of mixed growth,
of ash and hazel, alder and elder both,
glades cloudy with mist and rain
in almost tropical light.

Does money grow like leaves?
Old trees are daily felled for cash
or the corporate look as seen on television
(ranch or hotel, some such unnatural vision)
and laid low with a shrieking crash
by brash insensitives.

The rain forest in position
beside us, which has heard and seen
a like destruction where its neighbours stood,
foresees its own fate in the fallen wood
but stands firm, a resilient screen
against creeping desecration.

Unruly woods, the last
sanctuaries, as they were the first,
shelter the spirits of the natural realm
banished elsewhere, even from field and stream —
secreting, as worst comes to worst,
a life force from the past.

I go from tree to tree
after a downpour, noticing bright
drops on the branches, thirst of drinking veins,
earth voices, resinous breath of gasping pines,
and relish in renewed sunlight
their dense community.

What would we do, deprived
of these, what would the whole chain
of being be without their active sustenance?
No owls or foxes, only high finance
in a world of depleted oxygen
where once we used to live.

Triad for Shane MacGowan

1 A Rainy Night in Soho

A film crew have been working on a sordid
story of rape and murder in the brick lane
behind Ingestre Court, but pouring rain
has forced them to leave off and now it pours
on empty pavements and on blistered doors
unpainted since the Pogues first recorded
'A Rainy Night in Soho'. Two disorientated
drinkers, shoulders hunched against the wind,
head down uncertainly to Leicester Square
past sleeping shapes in corners of Greek St.
Tonight it's dismal even in the West End;
the squat's unheated and the cupboard bare.

2 Fairytale of New York

The drying-out clinics fill up in December;
once more it's that traumatic time of year.
The drugs are handed out in strict rotation
and the jakes locked except for diarrhoea.
She fell in love there, does she still remember,
and watched the snow on Seventh Avenue,
thrown up by buses, change to hail and rain
like bright tears on a grimy windowpane.
She soon checked out but what were we to do?
Steam drifted from underground and lights
danced in the river. We were hungry then
but happy too in the dark days and nights.

3 *Brought Up to Agitate*

Kirsty, 'brought up to agitate', sang along
with your now thirty-year-old punk Christmas song
for the last-minute shoppers splashing round
the supermarkets of some dirty old town.
A guy in the chipper swearing he was Elvis,
the girl in the video section, indeed all of us,
remembered her tough glamour in the eighties,
her pre-electric sound and brisk asperities,
when that Gonzalez' vicious speedboat ran
her down in the warm waters off Yucatan.
Her trenchant style is what we most recall
together with the names Seeger and MacColl.

To Hugh Haughton Retiring

I've never thought of you as 'retiring', Hugh —
just a few lines on your retirement though.
Because we know you're not the retiring sort
think of this juncture as the exciting start
of a new life-lease where you get around
to the great projects you've long entertained.

I've been retiring and retired out here
from the 'real world' for many a quiet year.
Who do I think I am? Tu Fu? Montaigne?
No, but such precedents do help sustain
a tactical retreat from the venal roar.
A few souls beat a path to the front door.

Houses are pricey and the tourists swarm
but if you're ever thinking about a warm
spot in the winter months to write *that book*
you could do worse than take another look
at these old places on the Atlantic coast
before the charm has been entirely lost.

We lose it by the month since the global crowd
can't take no for an answer and the loud
invaders wreck the peace they hope to find;
so better hurry and make up your mind.
At least come back and visit us in our
retirement on your once familiar shore.

An Age of Revolution

Earth *rotates* on its axis and *revolves*
in orbit round the sun. A little thought
in an uncosmic lifetime soon resolves
an obvious question of exact vocabulary
you hadn't really bothered to figure out,
the writing game can be so airy-fairy.

But you can revolve on an axis, yes you can,
like a turbine or a long-playing record.
It's revolutions drive the ship, the plane,
the disc; and it's a more interesting word
since they drive history besides, or did
before being taken up by the ad-men.

Tired of rotation, what we now require
is revolution, a whole age of it in fact
as in some previous, more exciting era —
an unmarketable but political solution
based on a simple model such as Brecht
proposed in the 'Babylonian Confusion';

for our own motives, base as they often are,
can change, and everyone already knows
the system's wrong, inhuman, though again
things get redacted so that even our
wisest forebears come to resemble us
in our own eyes and those of the unborn.

This isn't much of a 'poem', but a time
comes when you want to rough it up like him
and have your say in plain language for once.
It won't do to face the future with an oblique
and self-delighting virtuosity kick —
or is this the only practicable response?

On a Drowned Girl

(after Brecht)

After she perished and went drifting down
from streams to wider waters, towards the coast,
the wondrous opal of the heavens shone
as though to propitiate her sodden ghost.

Algae and weeds embraced her thighs and hands
so that she grew much heavier in limb.
Pike coolly nibbled at her pale flesh; plants
and river-life weighed down her final swim.

The evening sky grew dark as if with smoke
and night hung out its bright stars once again;
as became evident when daylight broke
dawn and dusk, night and day, would still go on.

While her bruised body decomposed down there
it happened that, very slowly, God too forgot her —
first her face, then her hands, and last her hair;
then she was bones like other bones in the water.

On Swimming in Lakes and Rivers

(after Brecht)

In bleaching summer when winds up below
breathe only in the leaves of the treetops
we want to swim in lakes and rivers like
the waterweed, dark haunts of hidden pike.
Bodies grow light in water. When an elbow
slips naturally from water into sky
a faint breeze dandles it distractedly,
mistaking it for a broken bough perhaps.

The sky at noon bestows an immense calm.
You blink when a swift suddenly goes by.
Cold bubbles rising where the mud is warm
show that a fish rose a split second ago.
Trunk and thighs, the muscles resting, lie
afloat on the surface, silently at one.
Casual perch and trout go flicking through;
you feel, burning beyond the trees, the sun.

At dusk, having grown lazy and apathetic
drifting so long, your limbs begin to fret.
You have to smash it up, with a good kick,
into blue ripples that dash hither and yon;
but it's best to hang in there until sunset
for then the pale sharkskin clouds will come,
greedy and sinister on pond and pine,
and everything take on its proper form.

All you've to do is lie flat on your back,
as if from force of habit, and play dead.
You needn't swim, no, just behave as though
you belong with the gravel on the river bed.

You have to look up at the sky and act
exactly as if a woman held you tight —
without commotion, like the dear Lord God
who swims his rivers in the evening light.

Brave New World

We put the clock back as the rule requires
so the dark nights start about five or so,
and rise betimes to a cold winter sun;
but turn it back half a century? Ah no,
not that again, the ignorant confusion
of growing up, and the mad student years.

Would I prefer the old times? Certainly not.
The further back you go the worse they get
though for that very reason life was simple,
slower, no high-tech frenzy for example
before the manic growth of corporate space
and playstations; but, sure, we know all this.

So face the brave new world with a wry grin
of tolerant irony, not of impotent hate;
but undermine the system from within
or hide away where any extraneous thought
derided by the regime is wrapped in mist
and mystery, if such places still exist.

Trump Time

1

Nineveh, Tyre and Carthage are long gone;
also Troy and the hanging gardens of Babylon.
Now Britain's empire is a thing of the past
and Angria too will have an end at last —
oh, not an end, but a slow decline at least.
Whitman and *Moby-Dick*, F. Scott Fitzgerald
will still be read, Gershwin and Satchmo heard,
movies downloaded; but the wider world
will think of other things, as it did once.
Hard rock and carpet bombing will be down,
Apple and Goldman Sachs down with the rest,
some peace and quiet once again in evidence.

2

Where a spring rises, in the little wood
of birch and sycamore beside the house,
I stand and listen to the undying source
whispering there. I'd travel if I could
through the lost ages to a distant time
when it was sacred to a pre-Christian god;
I'd tie a token on a thorn and climb
back to the present, sure in the belief
we can still touch the origins of life,
relish perspective, silence, solitude
far from the bedlam of acquisitive force
that rules us and would rule the universe.

3

Such things survive, beloved of poet and artist,
only where their despoilers haven't noticed —
in a yard or a hidden cove, out on the edge,
the rushy meadow and the fallow acre
ripe for development as industrial plant.
Serving as temple, shrine and sepulchre,
these places minister to the soul by dint
of radiating a strange air of privilege;
and here we live, not in a petulant rage
for world dominion but an inner continent
of long twilights shrouded in mist and rain,
the lasting features of our lost domain.

Ophelia

It started at nine in the morning as things do.
The eye of the cyclone remained out at sea
but we got the hard edge as it hit the coast
and, anti-clockwise, strove to devastate
a province; the lights failed and slates flew
while I sat it out here in 'excited reverie'
listening to climate change doing its work
with a stereophonic front of punitive rain.
Too much of water, fierce 'Ophelia', when
sea overwhelms our shaky earthworks. (Who
names storms, who names the winds and stars?)
No birds sing in this ominous half-dark.
We wait for daylight in the daylight hours
and, reading by candlelight as in other ages,
picture the whirling vortex, the wave surges
storming ashore; the roaring blitz of it.
It must be a sign of something, but of what?
The death of world civilization, I suppose,
and man-made climate is the evident cause —
which raises the grim question of what next?

   Now lights come on and the fridge shakes,
the phone speaks in a tone of huge relief;
whatever was under wraps returns to life.
Everything picks up with the sky at rest
and nothing to scare us for a while at least.
A bit like Key West in the strange aftermath,
whipping and dripping, the storm took a path
due north and died at last over Donegal,
just a high whistling wind like any gale,
nothing remarkable. Maybe Ophelia too
was nothing special, merely first of a new
series of weather events to be lived through.
Cyclones, of course, shouldn't come up this far
into our mild, predictable temperate zone
but rage down there below the blue horizon

like fire and pestilence; yet here they are,
one further import from the Angrian shore.
   Ophelia, royal girlfriend not the wind,
withdrew to nature like a sensible maid
but chose a flowing stream and willow shade —
a dubious option, not the best of choices,
and one she'd have refused in her right mind;
but it does get harder by the year to find
sanctuary from the clamour of crazed voices.
So shut the hatches, fill the shelves and hoard
candles against the dark time coming on
when hubris reaches for the infinite spaces
in a true cyclone spun by fatal industries
with this one filed as just an autumn breeze,
one of many before the real thing began.

Ivy

embraces fields of energy —
the ash, the yew, the hazel tree,
arbutus and pedunculate oak,
'Daphne with her thighs in bark'.
It drinks up its own nutrients, found
not in the trees but in the ground;
it breaks no branches, kills no flower,
content to leave them as they are.
Ivy, perennial victor, chokes
no sapling on the rise and makes
for some distinction, but beware
that resolute, brick-breaking power,
its choice of the most ailing elm
to cling and climb and overwhelm.
Still, its proud ancestral line
exalts it; ivy, like the vine
sacred to Dionysus, holds
its head up even when it crawls,
and even the bad poison kind —
so irritating but 'confined
to N. America' — though rare
has its own spiteful character.
    Common in hedges, woods and walls,
it flowers in autumn when supplies
of nectar dwindle, a late prize
for nectar-loving wasps and flies.
Stems can be inches thick and grow
up to a hundred feet or so:
considering their girth and height,
their aspiration towards the light,
they're almost trees in their own right.
Not an invasive species though.
Beloved of druids, like mistletoe,
it's known the love of poets too:

When the Ivy-tod is heavy with snow
And the Owlet whoops to the wolf below;
But in love again I will never be
'til apples grow on an ivy-tree.
    When all is ruin and the owl
looks on with an indifferent scowl,
rats and mosquitoes will abide
in the great cities where we died
and ivy cover earth and stone
with its dark cloak, oblivion,
rippling sedately in the sun.
Ivy will be the final flower
of life, as it has been before.
Bays and oak leaves? Not a chance.
When history bows to circumstance
it will be ivy that survives
the evidence of our vanished lives.

Being a Dog

The guardian spirit of the demesne
(cherished for her innocent mien,
her constancy and sense of fun,
a friendly word for everyone)
observes us with inquiring eyes
when we talk practicalities.
She fears she'd be misunderstood
and yet she'd join in if she could
since terriers think they're people too,
why not? When Cheeky looks at you
you're looking at a clever face
that registers your tone of voice
and notices each slight nuance
of grown-up intercourse at once.
    So what's it like, being a dog?
No inter-species dialogue
or dog-behavioural study shows
whatever it is we think she knows.
The stars, what does she make of those;
planes in the sky, cars in the drive
and the strange fact of being alive?
Maternity of course — her pup,
a daughter, Daisy, yielded up
to friends — upset her for a bit.
An operation went all right.
(She wore a lampshade round her neck
to not gnaw at the needlework.)
    Now rather a grand chatelaine,
she keeps watch on the lively train
of visitors to her property
and other dogs who live nearby.
She barks at dawn and late at night
around the gardens front and rear
to mark out her protectorate
for any dog who cares to hear

and take part in a dog debate.
She checks the gateposts with a sniff
and leaves her personal urograph,
'This is *my* terriortry; piss off'
or maybe 'Come at five o'clock
and, who knows, you could be in luck.'
The beanbag's there for her to doze,
the sunny porch on summer days,
her dish beside the kitchen door.
— *O Seligkeit der Kreatur!*
    But is there sorrow too, a sense
of scant, constrained experience,
nothing to wish beyond today,
poor thing? She never gets to say.
She never gets to formulate
the thoughts unspoken in her heart:
'Why are you people not like me
so we can bark together? Why
does it get cold in winter?' No,
these things are not for her to know,
nor the mad dreams of avarice
and toxic patriotism. It's best like this.

Thing Theory

The things reclaim their vibrant lives.
Scarves like magic carpets, gloves
like pigeons, take to the air in this
cool *Tatler* ad with amethyst
and agate, pearl and emerald
in flight round the consumer world:
'Things Come Alive' the caption says,
as theorists also do these days.
Books and boxes, tops and toys
keep to themselves and make no noise
except for the mute, stifled sound
of silence; but their thoughts rebound
on us the spectators who ascribe
cognition to their patient vibe.
We want the things to talk about
their life experiences, the brute
facticity of their being there,
the nuclear turbulence we share,
our common source in the 'primordial
bodies' (Lucretius); but the ordeal
of conversation is too much,
so we communicate by touch.

   What of the atoms? Do they blink
like fish in an aquarium tank
and look out at us looking in,
their obscure minds of wood and tin
responding in some curious fashion
to our intrusive inquisition?
Set the childish things aside,
the things in which we'd once confide
that understood and sympathized
(the model yacht so highly prized,
comics, Meccano, bric-à-brac,
the clockwork train and bits of track);
for these return as other things

with more sophisticated meanings —
as the high-tech and virtual play
that circumscribe our lives today,
the things you see discarded in
the rubbish heap and litter bin,
superfluous packaging and the rest
exhibiting with peculiar zest
as if aware of their objective
claim to our serious interest.
    Breathing air they also live
in the world, and maybe even strive
towards some sixth-dimensional zone
when we ourselves are dead and gone.
This copy of the *Tatler* too,
reduced to pulp, will know its true
value in time and pull its weight
as energy at some future date . . .

(unfinished)

Salisbury Avenue

(after Jean Rhys)

I used to live here once and played
with Tommy Burns and Anne McGlade
round garden sheds and open doors,
climbing trees and running races
in the immediate post-war years.
Now I revisit the old places
like an imagined camera eye
under a close and cloudy sky
at the approaching dinner hour.
A girl and boy are talking there,
convivial in an evening breeze
beside the latest four-by-four,
but when I speak they only gaze
through me as if I don't exist
even as a shadow or a ghost.
It's colder than it was before.
'I used to live here once', I say,
but the young people look away
shivering a bit, and turn to go,
not noticing me. So now I know.

A Dove in the House

On top of the pine a woodpigeon or rock dove
eyes the whole town and environs from above.
Rocking alone like the dove in Kierkegaard
and missing nothing, in garden or churchyard,
of life and death; circumspect, vigilant,
noticing everything from its vantage point,
it takes me back in time a great distance
to the strange year in my late adolescence

when we moved into a brand new housing estate.
There was no communal life up there on that
dismal hillside, it was so unfriendly.
You seldom saw another pedestrian, only
a car once in a while. There were no pets
in the area, no dogs on the road, no cats
about the doors; there *was* somebody though
who kept doves in his yard at a house below.

One afternoon, spring cleaning our new 'home',
my mother opened the windows. Coming home
from games I saw she'd had a great surprise
for there was an agitated look in her eyes
and in a back room, on a bed, sat a white dove.
We stood and watched it but it didn't move.
Withdrawing, we quietly left it on its own
and when we looked in later it was gone.

It had flown in by chance and just sat there
disoriented, returning our curious stare,
its feathers stirring in a gentle breeze
and sunlight shining in from April skies,
filling the room with summer. At the time
it felt as if a bright new paradigm
of communication had been demonstrated.
My mother and I never did talk about it

since we avoided things like peace and love,
but we tacitly agreed to consider the dove
as simply a bird escaped from a bird loft
half a mile down the road, and so we left
everything else unsaid. Did we remember
the olive leaf, the story of St. Columba?
Did we ever think of our visitor as a lost
soul, a mysterious gift, or a local ghost?

It *looked* like a ghost in that new bungalow —
a spirit materialized, for all we knew.
I'd seen the doves down at the other house
but for one to alight in ours was miraculous.
Was it there to enlighten us, to calm our fears,
to remind us, maybe, of certain quaint ideas?
And what did *it* think of our silent forum
before it headed back where it came from?

Although this might have been about religion,
not 'just' about a dove or a woodpigeon,
there's mystery enough in the bare fact
of reality without reaching for fantastic
notions of incarnation and revelation,
or so we fancy in our literal fashion;
still, we were silenced by that radiant bird
as though it had been sent to bring us word.

A North Light

(i.m. Basil Blackshaw, 1931-2016)

Divided up into flats, Glengormley House
was then an imposing and mysterious place
of artists, teachers and a retired colonel
with prominent local names (Agnew, McConnell)
who probably deplored our wretched new
'subsidy bungalows' going up down below.
I was over there on a number of occasions
like the young Pip in *Great Expectations*

except there was no beautiful girl in sight
and no strange boy wanting to start a fight,
only a quiet stable yard and a hen run.
The bay windows and gravel drive looked down
on *us*, the expanding suburb, the vast cemetery,
the lough as far as Whitehead and the sea.
A ring of elms shielded it from the wind;
the Cave Hill began in the fields behind.

I'd climb there and on summer afternoons
make out Dungannon, Slemish and the Mournes;
a few miles off, a high television mast
and the red-brick terraces of West Belfast,
birds in the back yards. I decided then,
despite what I'd inhaled with the oxygen,
province and country were identical places;
and so I avoided an 'identity crisis'.

The big-house people had included once
a fine painter whose intimate acquaintance
with dog and horse, their grain and character,
shone from his quick canvases, each actor
magical in a dawn mist. The wild sports
he favoured — hunting, racing and cockfights —

belied a gentle nature, widely known.
Strangely enough I never met the man

but his deft, living pictures make me think
of a mild tearaway who liked a drink
and the rough country life as it was once
before safety fascism assumed precedence.
He evidently enjoyed a whiff of sulphur
as those artists do who want to suffer
and reach the naked rim of raw creation
with everything in hard-won resolution.

The council houses with their favourite birds
holed up in pigeon lofts and garden sheds
exploded, famously, in a violent rage
and thick reaction; but the anarchic stage,
no longer news, now looks like history. Basil,
I picture you still gazing at your easel,
still working on the edge in love and fright,
everything fresh and true in a north light

beyond politics; and yet your raw material
was the radical resistance of the real
to a denatured world. Beasts of the field,
fowls of the air, dejected, live again
in your regard, albeit unknown to them.
We too, the heirs, are fortified and healed
by your organic art, and find release.
You were a great original; rest in peace.

Domestic Interior

You check your iPhone for the latest news
while I catch up with today's newspaper,
its chatty columnists and consensual views.
(Why can't they tell it as it really is?)
We groan together at the insanity but
there's not much that *we* can do about it.
Demonstrate and protest? A student caper
'cept they're too busy studying the game
of corporate finance to give a damn.
We played at radicalism in the old days;

some of us did at least, some of the time.
We still do, here in the lamplit living-room,
albeit unthreatened by the out-of-sight
disasters, happy in the western night
of known 'neutrality'. Which leaves us both
at peace to indulge a strictly selfless urge
with brush or pen, those urgent requisites
that exercise such influence on the age
saving the oceans and the rain forests,
the homeless and the unemployed. A moth

circles the lampshade like an ecstatic soul
from a dark place, enchanted by the gleam.
We're back in the black thirties of art deco,
fury and fascism, which a moth can't know.
Always the combat zone of heat and cold,
of light and darkness; always the same dream
of life and love, the same invidious forces:
deliberate ignorance and acquired odium.
These, if they win in the dark days to come,
will leave the pen and brush our sole resources.

Stroke of a duster and she's dust once more —
another soul gone to the shades, another

smudge on the hearthrug, shadow on the floor.
So much for enlightenment; so much for the fond
hopes of a soulful earth we entertained
in the old days before we understood.
Psyche, ghost of a butterfly, light-lover,
forgive our failure, constantly renewed,
to overcome the worst in them and us
whose own enlightenment is at best ambiguous.

Woodpigeons at the Grove

Not dove-demure, not sent to bring you word,
we humbly groan from our domestic wood
about material interests, just like anybody —
the leafy branch beside your quiet study,
enough cereal crops to appease appetite,
community by day, some peace by night.
We're the serene ones, dopey and content
to roost on the cool edge of a continent

for the duration of our natural lives.
We keep it simple; none of the species strives
after extraneous knowledge. The short glide
to farms and back again, our fantails spread
among the gobbling squabs, is flight enough.
Incurious about more adventurous stuff,
we never carried breaking news of old
and tactical dispatches from the field

or lived for racing as some others do.
Myth has ignored us, it prefers like you
to honour the slim doves, our glamorous cousins,
for its own time-honoured poetic reasons —
religious reasons — since we can't compare
with that white glow and aristocratic air;
so don't expect our dumpy kind to sport
the surplices of paragon and paraclete.

That said, when night has scoured the windy spaces
it's we who wake you with our grumbling voices.
Glance up at the pines, it will be us you see
perched on the topmost looking out to sea,
clapping our upswept wings with satisfaction.
But are we truly satisfied? Don't we itch
for the wide world? Nothing we know explains
the vague geography tingling in our veins.

You've read *Oiseaux* by St-John Perse, that rich
hymn to the Braque birds' far oceanic reach,
the 'asceticism' of flight, the great 'scythe wings',
'creative dreams'. While knowing about these things
instinctively, from instinct we sit tight —
from indolence, gravity, the force of habit.
Sure we'd shape up exploring, but another
shore is probably much like our own shore.

Crops ripen and granaries fill; we flock
to the gold grain spilt by a growling truck,
our idea of excitement. Real existence
consists of heat dispersing a dawn mist,
dew on the branches, branch water, sunlight
tempting the worms after a stormy night.
We have our music too, one simple phrase,
cro-roco-oh, relieving the long days.

Aren't we the comedians? As with geese and ducks,
puffins and penguins, our rum look provokes
a chuckle at the pompous chest and heavy
abdomen. You won't find us in Ovid
among the nightingales, for we're prosaic
creatures, neither heroic nor archaic
but worldly, self-confined to safety zones,
still dreaming of our once infinite horizons.

Acknowledgements

Acknowledgements are due to *The Irish Times*, the *TLS*, *The New Yorker*, *Irish Pages* and *Poetry Ireland Review* where some of these poems first appeared.

'Palinurus' and 'Montaigne' appeared in *New Selected Poems* (Gallery Books/Faber, 2016).

Sixteen poems appeared in *Rising Late,* a limited signed edition, with drawings and paintings by Donald Teskey (Gallery Books, 2017).